D0849852

Nature's Super Secrets

Why Do Animals Hibernate?

By Michael Ulinski

Gareth Stevens
Publishing

Please visit our website, www.garethstevens.com. For a free color catalog of all our high-quality books, call toll free 1-800-542-2595 or fax 1-877-542-2596.

Library of Congress Cataloging-in-Publication Data

Ulinski, Michael
        Why do animals hibernate? / by Michael Ulinski.
cm. – (Nature's super secrets)
Includes bibliographical references and index.
Summary: Brief text and photographs describe what happens when animals hibernate and how they prepare for their long winter sleep.
Contents: A long winter – Getting ready for bed – Who hibernates? – Welcome spring.
ISBN 978-1-4339-8176-0 (pbk.)
ISBN 978-1-4339-8177-7 (6-pack)
ISBN 978-1-4339-8175-3 (hard bound) –
1. Hibernation—Juvenile literature   [1. Hibernation]   I. Title
        2013
591.56/5—dc23

Published in 2013 by
Gareth Stevens Publishing
111 East 14th Street, Suite 349
New York, NY 10003

Designer: Nicholas Domiano
Editor: Sarah Machajewski

Photo credits: Cover Steve Bower/Shutterstock.com; p. 5 Lindsay Dean/Shutterstock.com;   p. 7 leonid_tit/Shutterstock.com; p. 9 Moritz Buchty/Shutterstock.com;
pp. 11, 21 Trudy Simmons/Shutterstock.com; pp. 13, 21 wim claes/Shutterstock.com;
pp. 15, 21 Wayne Lynch/All Canada Photos/Getty Images; pp. 17, 21 (chipmunk), 21(burrow) Margaret M Stewart/Shutterstock.com;
pp. 19, 21 Maksimilian/Shutterstock.com;

Printed in the United States of America

CPSIA compliance information: Batch #CW13GS: For further information contact Gareth Stevens, New York, New York at 1-800-542-2595.

Contents

Boldface words appear in the glossary.

A Long Winter

Winter is long and cold. People stay inside to keep warm. Do you know what happens to some animals that live outside? They hibernate! Hibernating means that an animal goes to sleep for the whole winter.

Animals hibernate because it's hard to find food in winter. The ground is **frozen** and covered in snow. If animals stayed awake, they would spend a lot of time looking for food that isn't there.

Getting Ready for Bed

It takes a lot of work to get ready to hibernate! Some animals eat a lot of food before winter comes. Others **collect** food and store it to eat later. All animals need food for the long winter ahead.

Animals' bodies slow down when they hibernate. They breathe very slowly. Their body **temperature** goes down, too. If their bodies work too much, they will need to eat more food than they have.

Who Hibernates?

All kinds of animals hibernate. Some sleep for months at a time. Others wake up every few days. Bears, chipmunks, and frogs are only a few animals that hibernate. Whether they're big or small, they all sleep for a long time!

13

When bears hibernate, they go into a very deep sleep. They don't even wake up to eat! They eat a lot of food in the summer and fall to get fat. The fat helps their bodies work while they sleep.

15

Chipmunks hibernate, too. They sleep in burrows. Burrows are holes under the ground. Chipmunks gather food during the summer and store it in their burrows. This gives them a lot to eat during the winter!

17

Can you **imagine** what it would be like to sleep in the mud? That's where frogs hibernate! The mud hides the frogs from fish and bigger animals. They stay safe there until spring.

Welcome Spring

Hibernating helps animals get through the long, cold winter. The animals wake up when spring comes. They're very hungry, so they leave their homes to find food and water. Next winter, they will hibernate again!

Where Do Animals Sleep?

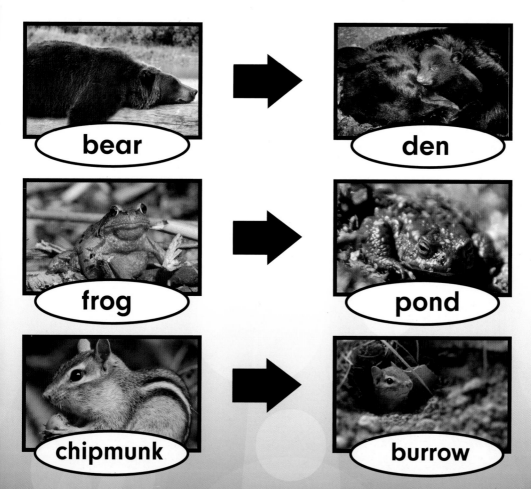

bear → den

frog → pond

chipmunk → burrow

Glossary

collect: to gather things together

frozen: made hard by the cold

imagine: to form a picture or idea of something in your mind

temperature: how hot or cold something is

For More Information

Books

Graham-Barber, Lynda. *The Animals' Winter Sleep.* Middletown, DE: Birdsong Books, 2008.

Nelson, Robin. *Hibernation.* Minneapolis, MN: Lerner Classroom, 2011.

Websites

Bear Facts — A Long Winter's Nap
www.kidzone.ws/lw/bears/facts.htm
Learn about bears and how they hibernate in winter.

Happy Hibernations!
kids.librarypoint.org/happy_hibernations
Find helpful information and fun activities about hibernation.

Top Ten Coolest Hibernating Animals
www.earthrangers.com/wildwire/top-10/top-ten-hibernating-animals/
Learn all about 10 different animals that hibernate.

Publisher's note to educators and parents: Our editors have carefully reviewed these websites to ensure that they are suitable for students. Many websites change frequently, however, and we cannot guarantee that a site's future contents will continue to meet our high standards of quality and educational value. Be advised that students should be closely supervised whenever they access the Internet.

Index